Through The Wilderness
WORKBOOK

*A guided spiritual adventure
through wilderness places.*

Carol A. Brown

LIGHTSMITH PUBLISHERS
Thorne Bay, Alaska

Copyright © 2018 by Carol A. Brown.

All rights reserved. No part of this publication may be reproduced, distributed or transmitted in any form or by any means, including photocopying, recording, or other electronic or mechanical methods, without the prior written permission of the publisher, except in the case of brief quotations embodied in critical reviews and certain other noncommercial uses permitted by copyright law. For permission requests, write to the publisher, addressed "Attention: Permissions Coordinator," at the address below.

Lightsmith Publishers
P.O. Box 19293
Thorne Bay, AK 99919
www.LightsmithPublishers.com

Ordering Information:
Quantity sales. Special discounts are available on quantity purchases by corporations, associations, and others. For details, contact the "Special Sales Department" at the address above.

Through The Wilderness WORKBOOK/ Carol A. Brown.
-- 1st ed.

ISBN: 978-1-944798-11-6

 Contents

Introduction

How To
Get the Most Out of This Workbook

1 Looking Around

2 Considering

3 Count Your Resources

4 Make Plans

5 PROVISION: A Closer Look

6 Three Steps Out (maybe four)

Other Books by Carol A. Brown

About the Author

Introduction

This *Through the Wilderness* workbook is an invitation to a spiritual adventure. It's a call to look again at the hard places in life with a different framework, a different perspective, a different set of lenses. Why are those hard things, the betrayals, the seeming failures, the pain and losses and the inexplicable craziness that came out of nowhere, permitted by the hand of a loving father! Is He allowing or is He—in incredibly miraculous ways— getting us out of situations we brought on ourselves?

Maybe He has had a better plan for us all along, and can use even these things to bring His dreams for us to pass. If only we would turn ourselves wholly over to Him for some "heavenly rehabilitation."

Stay with me! We prune fruit trees so they produce more fruit—and pruning is a savage, ruthless cutting away. Athletes lift heavier and heavier weights, and repetitively do the same exercise to develop muscle memory or to make muscles grow. We push promising athletes so they develop reflexes and we pile responsibilities on the son who shows promise. Is it inconceivable, then, that a holy God would use whatever adversity opposes us, to develop in us the spiritual muscles which are needed to love his presence and his will in our lives?

In my own journey "through the wilderness" with MS, I have discovered that God lovingly prepares the environment (the spiritual gym), but we must make the choice to exercise the faith that makes us want to spend time with God and praise him, regardless of our outward circumstance.

I am right there with Paul when he says, *"Not that I have already obtained all this, or have already been made perfect, but I press on to take hold of that for which Christ Jesus took hold of me."(Phil 3:12)* We are always a work in progress until we stand before our King!

In this deeper study of my devotional memoir, *Through The Wilderness*, I will be guiding you through some of the activities and assignments the Lord gave to me in order to more fully understand myself, and how that related to what I was going through. While there may be different experiences for different people and situations, a lot of the basic steps are the same.

In the following pages we will touch on some of the deeper issues of a wilderness experience through the use of:

- **SURVIVAL TIPS**

- **QUESTION / ANSWER SESSIONS** with the Holy Spirit
- **WORD STUDIES**
- **SCRIPTURE GUIDES**
- **BRIEF COMMENTARIES** about the chapter subjects
- **NEW COMMENTARY** on a few issues not included in the book
- **THREE-STEP METHOD** on how to get guidance
- **JOURNAL PAGES** at the end of each chapter that you can record your personal thoughts and conversations with the Lord on. Extra pages have been provided in case you might want to stop back for a "raincheck" now and again, so it's a good idea to date each entry.

Each chapter ends with questions that invite the reader to go deeper—to be ruthlessly honest with themselves and with God—and allow God to correct what is out of order or alignment.

So, come join me for a workout in your own "wilderness gym." Maybe you're struggling through a hard place, too, or going through some other fire of affliction. If so, your spiritual muscles are getting a workout. I believe it is God's design to make you strong, healthy, and more in love with him than ever, no matter

what the world tries to throw at you.
   So, grab your gear and come along!

Carol

How To Get The Most
Out Of This Workbook:

BEGIN WITH PRAYER, ask the Lord to teach you something from this time with Him today.

Read the SURVIVAL TIP, the brief commentary, the SCRIPTURE GUIDE, and the WORD STUDY. Then take a few minutes to think about those things.

Ask the Lord to open your eyes where the personal questions apply to you, and how you should deal with them. Then read the questions and spend some time listening to the Holy Spirit.

Write down in the journal pages anything you would like to be reminded of or remember about this encounter.

THANK THE LORD for meeting with you, today.

• ***SURVIVAL TIP:*** *If you suddenly find yourself lost and have no idea where you are—stop moving. Sit down somewhere and give yourself time to calm down. Then take a good look around to familiarize yourself with where you are, and make a plan for what you can do.*

1
Looking Around

The first chapter of my book, *Through the Wilderness,* which is titled: *Different, Not Ruined,* speaks to the identity struggle that multiple sclerosis—or trauma of any kind— precipitates. In that short monologue the conclusion is reached that even though the attack had definitely made life different from what it was, my life (or your life) is not thereby ruined. It cannot be ruined unless we agree with that assessment.

• SCRIPTURE GUIDE

"I call heaven and earth to record this day against you, that I have set before you life and death, blessing

and cursing: therefore choose life, that both you and your children may live."

(Deuteronomy 30:19)

• WORD STUDY

SURVEY: (of a person or their eyes) look carefully and thoroughly at (someone or something), especially so as to appraise them. Or, to examine and record the area and features of (an area of land) so as to construct a map, plan, or description.

To survey something is etymologically to "oversee" it. The word comes via the Anglo-Norman word *surveier* derived from the medieval Latin word *supervidēre*, a compound verb formed from the prefix super—or "over"— and the verb *vidēre* "see"
    (source of English is: view, vision, etc).

  • **CONSIDER** the following three questions.

By looking at the trauma that put you into the wilderness, what part of your life was the enemy trying to ruin?

The Lord wants to redeem you from this devastation

and restore you in such a way that you thrive, which is much more than just functionality!

- **SCRIPTURE GUIDE**

"Beloved, I wish above all things that you may prosper and be in health, even as your soul prospers."

(3 John 1:2)

Ask the Holy Spirit to help you see a glimpse of what that might be in your life.

Can you come into agreement with what God shows you?

- **JOURNAL:** Take a moment to jot anything you would like to remember on the journal pages that follow.

Journal Pages

SURVIVAL TIP: *Think. Put the feeling of panic aside. Stay calm, and try to approach the situation rationally. Consider what made you realize you were lost in this wilderness—a compass reading, a trail that suddenly disappeared, or the absence of a landmark that you are supposed to see. Stay put while you think and assess the situation—moving is more likely to make things worse.*

2
Considering

As I continued to work through the identity struggle, I learned the importance of "shelf time." It is an opportunity to still the clamor our lives can have by going inward into Jesus and learning how to plumb that relationship. To develop intimacy with Him and begin to see things from His perspective rather than our own. It is a time of drying out and becoming seasoned so that we can endure the fire of what the Lord calls us into. The next level. So that we do not explode; so that we can come through this fire without destroying self or others.

- **SCRIPTURE GUIDE**

"You intended evil against me, but God used it for good, to accomplish what is now being done...and to save the lives of many others..."

(Genesis 50:20)

WORD STUDY

- **VISA**: A visa is etymologically something "seen." the word comes via French visa from Latin vīsa, literally "things seen," a noun use of the neuter plural form of the past participle of vidēre "see" (source of English vision, visit, etc). The notion underlying the word is that a visa is a note or other mark made on a passport to signify that it has been officially "seen" or examined.

- **CONSIDER** the following three questions.

Gases in clay that goes into the fire before being fully dried explodes and can potentially destroy all the other pieces in the kiln. **Ask the Lord to reveal any such air pockets there may be in your life while you are on your drying shelf.**

Ask Holy Spirit to help you see or acknowledge whether you are submitting to the purposes of this season and developing intimacy with Jesus or if you

are indulging in self-pity and comparison.

Ask Him to show you what true submission to His purposes looks like.

Unresolved issues can explode when we are moved into positions with responsibilities for which we are not well enough seasoned to carry. If we look at being on the shelf as a time of seasoning and strengthening, we can also see it as a place of protection during this process.

• SCRIPTURE GUIDE

"After you have suffered a little while, the God of all grace, who has called you to his eternal glory in Christ, will himself restore, confirm, strengthen, and establish you"

(1 Peter 5:10)

Ask the Holy Spirit to work in your situation to bring these things about.

Can you agree to let him change what was meant for evil and do a new work in you?

- **JOURNAL:** Take a moment to jot anything you would like to remember on the journal pages that follow.

Journal Pages

Carol A. Brown

Through The Wilderness WORKBOOK

SURVIVAL TIP: *Observe. Check out your surroundings and consider what landmarks might help you situate yourself. Compare your observations to your map, which could help you get reoriented. Consider how the weather looks, what time of day it is, and what supplies you have on hand. All of these factors will help you develop an action plan.*

3
Count Your Resources

As I continued on my eyes saw missed opportunities, goals and visions thwarted. I regretted all that would not be. It ate away at the tiny bit of energy I did have…until I saw with God's eyes. Right there is the parable! Ask God to view your trouble through His eyes; then you will have a proper perspective and understand the bigger picture!

MS robbed me of energy and motivation, but joy restores it. Joy energizes—it is the source of strength—it literally causes our physical brain to activate the energy to do life. Having joy, I am able to catch a vision that will channel the energy that joy activates!

• SCRIPTURE GUIDE

"...this day is holy to our Lord. And do not be grieved, for the joy of the Lord is your strength."

(Nehemiah 8:10)

• WORD STUDY

When I decided to do a word study of vision, and saw that is part of the word "provision," I also included it here.

PROVIDE: The –vide of provide goes back to Latin *vidēre* "see" (source of English vision), which is a long way from the English verb's main present-day meaning, "supply." Its Latin ancestor *providēre*, formed with the prefix prō- "before," meant "foresee" – a sense which survived into English: "evident and sufficient signs, whereby may be provided and foreseen the *aborcement* (abortion) before it comes."
t already in Latin it had moved on to "exercise foresight by making preparations." and this formed the basis of the later "supply." Other English descendants of *prōvidēre* include improvise, provident (a close relative of prudent), provision, *proviso*, and purvey.

• **CONSIDER** the following three questions.

Ask the Lord to give you a vision that will channel the joy that activates. Invite Him to be the driving force in your life from now on, your anchor and grounding so that your history and destiny will stay on course.

Ask Holy Spirit to reveal any little fissures of distrust that present weak spots where the enemy could break through...regrets are the tell-tale signs.

Ask the Holy Spirit to show you a plain path through your wilderness, and help you to believe He will provide all you will need along this journey.

- **SCRIPTURE GUIDE**

"Teach me thy way, oh Lord, and lead me in a plain path, because of mine enemies."

(Psalm 27:11)

"... and this is the victory that overcomes the world, even our faith."

(1 John 5:4)

- **JOURNAL:** Take a moment to jot anything you would like to remember on the journal pages that follow.

Journal Pages

SURVIVAL TIP: *Plan. Brainstorm potential next steps and decide on a plan. You might choose to camp out overnight, waiting for daylight to make your next move. If you feel confident that you can get back on track, leave a trail marking the path you take (like a breadcrumb trail, but use rocks or some other marker).*

4
Make Plans

My life shattered in a million pieces because of the damage from the attack that catapulted me into my wilderness. Slowly the Lord gave me value, worth and purpose. Through it all, I came to understand the beauty He built into me and that this beauty calls people to Him.
I am His voice calling to others lost in their wilderness; a light to guide them "home."

The Lord knows the lines along which we will break. He gathers all our pieces and lovingly rearranges them with Christ at the center, so that as works of God's art we refract His Glory which He puts in us in glorious beauty and lively color for all to see. Being a work of God's art calls people to life, calls them "home."

- **SCRIPTURE GUIDE**

"But we all, with open face beholding as in a glass the glory of the Lord, are changed into the same image from glory to glory, even as by the Spirit of the Lord."

(2 Corinthians 3:18)

- **WORD STUDY**

IVISIT: Visit is one of a large family of English words that go back to Latin *vidēre* "see." This in turn was descended from the Indo-European base *woid-, weid-, wid-*, which also produced English wise and wit. Other members of the family include envy, revise, survey, video, view, visa, visage, visible, vision, visor, vista, and visual. Visit itself comes from the Latin derivative *visitāre*, which meant literally "go to see."

- **CONSIDER** the following three questions.

When you cannot see any of the beauty God has in store for you, ask Him to let you see through His eyes.

If you still cannot see, ask Holy Spirit to reveal what is keeping you from seeing through the eyes of

heaven.

Thank Him for the privilege of being part of refracting the glory and beauty of Jesus, and for making something even more beautiful out of your life than what you originally planned.

SCRIPTURE GUIDE

"...eye hath not seen, nor ear heard, neither have entered into the heart of man, the things which God hath prepared for them that love him."

(1 Corinthians 2:9)

JOURNAL: Take a moment to jot anything you would like to remember on the journal pages that follow.

Journal Pages

5

PROVISION

A closer look.

Our loving father has looked into the future and "foreseen" what we would need not only to survive but, to thrive. He has carefully guided our history so that we are equipped to wring the optimum benefit from these experiences. Here are some special promises He has made to help us truly believe this.

Scriptures:

"I will be your God throughout your lifetime—until your hair is white with age. I made you, and I will care for you. I will carry you along and save you."

(Isaiah 46:4)

Psalm 23

"The Lord is my shepherd; I lack nothing.
He makes me lie down in green pastures, He leads me beside quiet waters,
He refreshes my soul. He guides me along the right paths for his name's sake.

Even though I walk through the darkest valley, I will fear no evil, for you are with me; Your rod and Your staff, they comfort me.
You prepare a table before me in the presence of my enemies. You anoint my head with oil; my cup overflows.
Surely your goodness and mercy will follow me all the days of my life, and I will dwell in the house of the Lord forever."

"This is my resting place for ever and ever; here I will sit enthroned, for I have desired it. I will bless her with abundant provisions; her poor I will satisfy with food. I will clothe her priests with salvation, and her faithful people will ever sing for joy."

(Psalm 132:14-16 NIV)

"And my God will meet all your needs according to the riches of his glory in Christ Jesus."

(Philippians 4:19 (NIV)

> NOTE: The Greek word translated as "will meet" all your needs is "*ple-re-o*" which carries the meaning of accomplish, accomplishment, to fulfill, to complete, carry out to the full—this is provision! He will take care of us even in the wilderness.

"Cast your cares on the Lord and he will sustain you; he will never let the righteous be shaken."

(Psalm 55:22)

"For forty years You sustained them in the wilderness; they lacked nothing, their clothes did not wear out nor did their feet become swollen."

(Nehemiah 9:21)

"Cast all your anxiety on Him because He cares for you."

(Psalm 18:2)

"The Lord is my rock, my fortress and my deliverer; my God is my rock, in whom I take refuge, my shield and the horn of my salvation, my stronghold."

(1 Peter 5:7)

"No one will be able to stand against you all the days of your life. As I was with Moses, so I will be with you; I will never leave you nor forsake you."

(Joshua 1:5)

"Nehemiah said, 'Go and enjoy choice food and sweet drinks, and send some to those who have nothing prepared. This day is holy to our Lord. Do not grieve, for the joy of the Lord is your strength."

(Nehemiah 8:10)

"Trust in him at all times, you people; pour out your hearts to him, for God is our refuge."

(Psalm 62:8)

"But I will sing of your strength, in the morning I will sing of your love; for you are my fortress, my refuge in times of trouble."

(Psalm 59:16)

"I will say of the Lord, "He is my refuge and my fortress, my God, in whom I trust."

(Psalm 91:2)

"I lie down and sleep; I wake again, because the Lord sustains me."

(Psalm 3:5)

"The Lord sustains them on their sickbed and restores them from their bed of illness."

(Psalm 41:3)

"Restore to me the joy of your salvation and grant me a willing spirit, to sustain me."

(Psalm 51:12)

"The Lord sustains the humble but casts the wicked to the ground."

(Psalm 147:6)

"For we are God's handiwork, created in Christ Jesus to do good works, which God prepared in advance for us to do."

(Ephesians 2:10)

"And this is my prayer: that your love may abound more and more in knowledge and depth of insight, so that you may be able to discern what is best and may be pure and blameless for the day of Christ, filled with the fruit of righteousness that comes through Jesus Christ—to the glory and praise of God."

(Philippians 1:9-11 NIV)

I had no idea that the Lord's plan was for me to become a writer. I knew that I loved to teach, to see the light in a student's eyes as understanding dawned—I loved it! So, I learned what I needed to become a teacher. I submitted to the list of hurdles society raises and acquired a certain skill set that enabled me to meet the requirements for doing what I was good at.

It never occurred to me that the skill set for teaching was also needed to be a writer. God used my passion to prepare me to write. I learned to type and now when inspiration hits I can fly across the keyboard and record it. I learned sentence structure and grammar to pass it on to students, but it also prepared me to write clean manuscripts later. Everyone needs an editor and proofreader, but knowing the language well makes the work easier and quicker.

So, now I would ask you to look at your own history and see if you can find ways your heavenly Father looked into your future and provided—beforehand—for your wilderness time. Discover how wonderfully He provided training and skills that you would need now.

List your training and skills:

1_____

2_____

3_____

4_____

5_____

6

THREE STEPS OUT
(maybe four)

Or *how to get to the Promised Land in under forty years!*

Ever wonder if "the wilderness" by definition is a forty year gig? Do I have to go round the mountain yet again? Another time? How can I learn from my own and others' mistakes so I don't have to repeat them? What could I do differently and arrive at my promised land in something less than forty years?

I submit to you that incorporating these three steps into your life will dramatically change your wilderness experience.

These steps are not in any order of importance. We humans are so terribly logical-sequential. Step one has to come before step two…that's just the way the numbers go. However, it is The Lord God who has brought you out here to the wilderness…for some reason known only to Him. So we are talking about a relationship with the Creator of the Universe here, and human sense of time and sequence is irrelevant to Him. Or perhaps I should say that God is outside of our dimension. He is outside of time as we know it and He is unaffected by the way we sequence information. He did design us to function and think the way we do. He put us within time and understands our time and logical sequencing. Humanity, on the other hand, was not designed to comprehend God; we were designed to relate to Him and enjoy Him.

When the Lord begins your formation into the image of Christ He works all three of these steps at the same time. It really messes with your mind! You want to focus on one or two things at a time but it does not bother Him in the least to work all of them. You may have seen three dimensional chess or checkers games; it's sort of like that. God gets it all going at the same time and keeps track of each piece. But to consider the steps, you must operate within your own sequencing—just remember that number one is no more or less important than numbers two and three.

Step 1
Obedience

Obedience is action. The children of Israel had a problem with this one. Although obedience is action, it is action based upon trust and a firm belief in the goodness of God's nature; the belief that regardless of circumstances, He is working all to your good.

He protects and provides; He is wise. He knows what He is doing and where He is taking you. Israel's kids did not know this, so teaching the concepts and working them down to the heart and reflex level was on God's agenda as He brought them into the wilderness. They would not be distracted by the nine to five dead end job they had back in Egypt. They only had to put one foot in front of the other and learn about the nature of God. So maybe that is why He brings you and me into the wilderness—to teach us a thing or two about Himself without distraction?

To obey is to act on God's directive(s) whether or not it is convenient; whether or not you understand, or even whether you like what you have been asked or told to do. You act because of who God is and you trust His character and nature. You act because you trust His Word that all things will work out for your good (Romans 8:28). You do what He asks because He has not failed to provide and protect in the past. Or, you can act without trusting or understanding—just do it because God said so!

Obedience does not negate your questions or need for answers. God is not bothered by questions; however, the questions need to follow "Yes, Lord." Here are some questions I ask—quite often, actually.

What do You want me to do? What do You mean by...? What exactly are You saying? Many times a clarifying question is important. For example, if the Lord says, "Wait on Me" does He mean that you are to wait on Him as in serve Him, or does He mean to stop what you are doing? Clarification is appropriate, but ask for it after having accepted His request or command.

When is a relevant question, too. Moving too quickly can be as disastrous as not moving or moving too slow. Gideon is a classic example of this. (Judges 6 and following) He was told to wait until he had the right number of men and heard certain sounds and then to move.

God once asked my husband and family to move without giving us a destination. After we went as far as He indicated He would give another instruction. We would follow it, and so on until the day came when our next assignment was clear. It took over five months. He took us through a very narrow place where we could not see the final outcome before settling us in "a good land." We had to walk in faith, move at His command and hold to the foundation of that faith—that God is good and His purposes are to bless us and give us a hope and a future.

How can this be? That was Mary's question and also the question Zechariah, father of John the Baptist asked. (Luke 1) They asked the same question but Mary was not rebuked and Zechariah was. I believe there was an attitudinal difference. Mary was simply confounded, but was Zechariah cynical or bitter. Was the attitude "Yeah, right! At my age? Ha! How can these things be?" I can hear an underlying statement of, "You have got to be kidding!" There was some unbelief mixed in with the question.

How do you want me to pray? How do I do this? These are appropriate clarifying questions as long as asked in an attitude of obedience….as you are packing your suitcase or your tool box. Ask it as you are moving to carry out the directive.

Why is another question that can get you into trouble. If the question is asked while moving to obey you are less likely to become mired by it. But if you ask what, how and why as a means to buy time, as a delaying tactic because you do not want to obey, you will have difficulties. If you ask so that you can judge the merits of God's idea, then it will probably not go well! God may not give an answer because He knows you would not understand even if He told you. Some answers are beyond your capacity to understand.

The finite human design does not include the capacity to comprehend the infinite, the eternal. Like children stuck in the "Why?" stage you become agitated and upset when you do not hear or see an answer, when the problem may be a lack of capacity or ability to understand the answer. Parents are not the only ones who say, "Because I said so!"

Countless times when knitting a garment I objected to the directions because they did not make sense to me. I tried to figure out the pattern and do it a different way that "made more sense." Until finally in frustration I followed the directions without deviation or question, whether it made sense to me or not… and then the pattern emerged. Once I followed the instructions fully and saw *how* the pattern emerged, I could understand. Understanding followed the obedience.

Life is similar to that. The pattern of beauty and

purpose that God is weaving into the tapestry of your life may not be visible to you while you are going through it. Often in retrospect you can see what God was doing, where He was leading. Life does not have to make sense to you. Nowhere is it written, "Thou shalt understand!" But the command to obey is plainly written:

Here are some scriptures to reinforce these things.

*Exodus 34:11: "**Obey** what I command you today."*

*Leviticus 25:18: "Follow my decrees and be careful to **obey** my laws, and you will live safely in the land."*

Numbers 13 is the account of the Israelites giving a bad report when Moses had the leaders spy out The Promised Land.

They caused fear in the people so that they did not enter the first time around. When they realized the error of their ways they resolved to go in and fight and were soundly beaten; they had gone without Moses or God. The effort was borne out of remorse—they were sorry they didn't obey, but sorry because of the consequences rather than sorry because they hurt the heart of their God who loves them dearly. A kid about to be punished will say, "I'm going, I'm going! I'll do it!" But delayed obedience does not bless the parent. Delayed obedience on our part does not please our Heavenly Father either.

That bit of disobedience (borne of the fear of man) cost them forty years of wandering in the desert until all of that unbelieving generation died. The Lord did not take disobedience lightly. All those men on the spy team who spread the bad report were struck down by a plague. Only Caleb and Joshua survived. God was ready to "nuke" the whole lot of them and would have if Moses had not interceded! God does not change; He is of the same opinion in regard to obedience today. I am not suggesting that God is a meanie sitting up there on a cloud with a fly swatter ready to clobber us but I am saying that foot dragging does not please Him; obedience does.

The New Testament is also filled with the admonition to obey. Here are just a few:

*Matthew 28:20: "...and teaching them to **obey** everything I have commanded you. And surely I am with you always, to the very end of the age."*

*John 14:23: "Jesus replied, "Anyone who loves me will **obey** my teaching. My Father will love them, and we will come to them and make our home with them."*

Romans 2:13: "For it is not those who hear the law who are righteous in God's sight, but it is those who

***obey** the law who will be declared righteous."*

Step 2
Submission

Submission is tied in with obedience. Submission is the heart attitude and obedience or disobedience is the outward expression of the attitude of the heart. I believe that murmuring, grumbling and complaining fall in the category of disobedience born of a heart not submitted. These behaviors reveal an underlying discontent, dissatisfaction and unbelief—a negative attitude—that results in half-hearted obedience and slowness to move to action.

As I reread the story of the Exodus and the children of Israel's trek through the wilderness I was astonished at the amount of grumbling under the breath. Something was wrong at every turn. Moses was gone too long, there was no water, there was no food, they were tired of manna, who did Moses think he was anyway…we should have stayed in Egypt, died in Egypt…grouse, grouse, grouse! It was a litany…same tune second verse…same tune thirty-third verse!

Exodus 14:10-12: As Pharaoh approached, the Israelites looked up, and there were the Egyptians, marching after them. They were terrified and cried out to the Lord. [11] They said to Moses, "Was it because there

were no graves in Egypt that you brought us to the desert to die? What have you done to us by bringing us out of Egypt? [12] *Didn't we say to you in Egypt, 'Leave us alone; let us serve the Egyptians'? It would have been better for us to serve the Egyptians than to die in the desert."*
"We should have stayed in Egypt."

God delivered them by the crossing of the Red Sea. After the miracle they feared God and put their trust in Him. God was willing to work with the "seeing is believing" attitude.

In Exodus 15:22 it says: *"So the people **grumbled** against Moses, saying, "What are we to drink?"* They found water at Marah but it was bitter so God had Moses throw a piece of wood into the water and it became sweet. Here again the specter of lack of provision filled them with fear. They forgot how He saved them from the Egyptians and could not generalize that God's power to protect was enough to also provide.

*Exodus 16:1-3: In the desert the whole community **grumbled** against Moses and Aaron.* [3] *The Israelites said to them, "If only we had died by the Lord's hand in Egypt! There we sat around pots of meat and ate all the food we wanted, but you have brought us out into this desert to starve this entire assembly to death."*

They grumbled about the food so God gave them manna and quail.

Exodus 17:3: "They traveled from the desert of Sin to Rephidim and there the people were thirsty for *water, and they **grumbled** against Moses. They said, 'Why did you bring us up out of Egypt to make us and our children and livestock die of thirst?"*

God did not rebuke them for being thirsty but He did hear the grumbling. He directed Moses to strike the rock with his rod and water came out.

In Exodus 20:19 (at Mt. Sinai): The people asked Moses to speak to them rather than God directly. The smoke and thunder and lightning on the mountain made them fear that if God spoke directly to them they would die. "Just tell us and we will do it!"

Exodus 32: Moses was taking so long on Mt. Sinai that the people made a golden calf and began to sacrifice and worship. Part of the judgment was that the Levites were directed to indiscriminately kill approximately three thousand people!

Numbers 11: When they complained, the fire of God destroyed the outer edges of the camp.

Numbers 14:22: God says, *"You have disobeyed me ten times!"* (Notice that He said that in the context of grumbling?)

Those who died off were from the age of twenty on up so when they did enter the land, it was as a youthful people. These young people had spent their entire lives roaming the desert. This made them physically healthy. The older generation was a fear based group; the younger ones had become a love based group. Relationship based on fear is neither rewarding nor fulfilling; whereas those based on love are. They are also much more enduring.

Matthew 21:28-32: In the parable of the two sons Jesus reveals God's heart on the matter of obedience and submission. The first son is forthright and simply says, "No." The second son says "Yes" but does not obey. When Jesus asked the disciples which of the two did what the father wanted they had no trouble identifying the obedient son.

Jesus only said what He heard the Father say. So that says to me that Father God would rather you speak to Him honestly and openly what is in your heart. It is better to be truthful and say "No" and then repent of that rebellious attitude than to be sneaky or two-faced. God wants us to be honest in our relationship with Him.

One of the best examples of the attitude of submission that I have heard was summed up on a blog by Arthur Burke, for the Sapphire Leadership Group. He put it this way: "I never would have written the script this way, but since You have, I am choosing to believe You see something I don't see, and from Your point of view this is good and right and loving. Therefore, I celebrate Your wisdom from my place of limited perspective." There is no question of God's goodness or intentions, nor His ability and willingness to provide and protect. You can admit to God that you do not understand, that you would prefer to understand and still not let that lack of understanding affect your obedience.

Step 3
Worship and Remember

When I taught English as A Second Language I learned that when under stress a learner will revert to the old language pattern. It didn't mean that he or she had not learned English, or had forgotten what he learned. It simply meant that they were under stress. Take away the stress and the learning resurfaces.

For example, the Japanese student under stress would say "liva" meaning "river." In Japanese there is no meaningful difference between "l" and "r." They do not distinguish between those two sounds; in essence the two sounds mean the same thing to them. Or, it might be
a grammatical issue. A Japanese girl excited about going shopping might say, "I am going to shopping." She knows that the correct way to say it is "I am going shopping." But in her excitement she does not self-edit and reverts to the Japanese language structure.

Under stress you and I forget (momentarily) what we know. Over and over again the new things the children of Israel learned would slip; they would forget in the face of a new stress and revert to the old ways. So, God repeated Himself over and over again, *"When you enter the land I swore to give to your Fathers...."* And then gave instructions that would help them remember. He was building into their culture the reflexes to remember and to worship even under stress. To remember and worship in spite of stress and because of stress. (See Deuteronomy 6) God gave them instructions to talk about the Exodus, to tell their children, to memorize their scriptures and gave them festivals to celebrate God's goodness. People need to be reminded; God knew that and put many reminders into the culture to help the people remember and worship.

Shortly after the MS attack I had a physical therapist come to my home and we devised exercises for every room in the house. When I stood at the sink I did one exercise; when I passed through the doorway I did a different one. The living room had its set of exercises and so on so that I was continually exercising damaged nerves and muscles. The room itself became the reminder. After a time exercise became a reflex and I no longer had to think about what to do. That's how God wants your worship and remembering His goodness, His protection and provision to be—to come automatically, as a first response.

God wants you to develop the reflex of worship. The sooner you develop that reflex of worship and remembering what He has done and Who He is, the sooner you will see a shift. Problems and difficulties will not necessarily disappear, but the way you deal with them will and the effect you have on others as you go through the difficulty will be different.

My proposal is that when you bump up against life's difficulties or when you realize that you are in a wilderness time *bust out in worship and praise*—even if you don't feel like it. God highly values the sacrifice of praise.

Read the Psalms aloud if you cannot sing. King David got to the depth and expressed it beautifully. There is something about praise in the difficult places that brings changes. For example, see the response of Paul and Silas in Acts 16:16. Emotions begin to come in line with the truth of the praise; it calms the raging emotion and then you can remember.

"I remembered thy judgments of old, O Lord; and have comforted myself." (Psalm 119:52 KJV)

"I have remembered thy name, O Lord, in the night, and have kept thy law." (Psalm 119:55 KJV)

Talk to yourself. *"Why, my soul, are you downcast? Why so disturbed within me? Put your hope in God, for I will yet praise him, my Savior and my God."* (Psalm 42:5 KJV)

Your loving Father does know how you learn best. What you are going through is undoubtedly hard but I think that worship will calm the racing thoughts and raging emotions enough so that you can submit and obey. The effect of submission and obedience is strength of spirit, mind and emotions—maturity. It will also strengthen and deepen your relationship with Jesus.

Worship, submission and obedience are transformational. Time with Jesus in the wilderness is transformational, so much so that people will do a double take when they see you.

"Who is this coming up from the wilderness like a column of smoke, perfumed with myrrh and incense made from all the spices of the merchant? (Song of Songs 3:6)

You won't even look like your old self!

Build Endurance and Perseverance

Building endurance and perseverance is actually one of the effects of steps one through three but I think it needs to be part of this piece as an encouragement. When your base line is that God is good and all life's experiences are filtered through His hands of love, your approach to difficulty is different. With a base line of love, you can embrace the difficulties much as an athlete embraces rugged discipline in training and conditioning for a competition. The training hurts; the muscles and lungs ache. The body may scream for relief but he or she pushes that little bit more and the body responds by developing more muscle and more capacity.

Spiritually speaking, God wants each of us to develop spiritual muscle, spiritual authority and capacity. It is in love that He turns difficulties in your life into something beneficial for you. He will not allow the trials of life to crush you if you turn them completely over to Him. Overcoming adversity not only changes us, but becomes a hope-igniting testimony for others. It could even be that looking at adversity more like qualifying trials which reveal what needs to be shored up and strengthened in us could also get us through them faster.

The children of Israel did not actually need a physical fitness program. They had had one for four hundred years! Making bricks is hard manual labor. Their bodies were in good shape already, but the spirit still needed to push against the different issues that developed on that journey.

They needed to have Egypt's values and idolatry flushed from their minds and spirits as well as their bodies. They needed to learn a personal relationship with their God. This trek through the wilderness could be used to develop strength of spirit, emotions, and mind so that their reflex response to God might be loving worship, praise, submission, trust and obedience. I submit to you that your wilderness hike—and mine—have those same possibilities. The details will differ according to each individual, but the overall outcome is the same: to create sons and daughters with a striking resemblance to Jesus.

The wilderness stretches you physically, emotionally, mentally and spiritually. It will trim you down in places and bulk you up in others. Yet, it is still up to us whether we will stay there or move on. Jesus knows His way through the wilderness—He has been there. And we can follow Him out. But it is the following and staying close that truly transforms us.

It makes us more like Him.

Other Books By
Carol A. Brown

For Adults:

The Mystery of Spiritual Sensitivity

Highly Sensitive

For Children:

Sassy Pants Learns The Hard Way

Sassy Pants Learns How To Make Amends

Sassy Pants Learns About Strange Creatures

About the Author

Carol A. Brown is the author of six books, including the popular Mystery of Spiritual Sensitivity, which has been translated into four languages. She is also the author of the Sassy Pants Learns series, in which she distills some of the more mysterious truths of life into the language of children. Carol and her husband live in Alaska, and have been in Christian ministry for many years. They have two daughters, five grandchildren, and a great-grandson. You can get in touch with her through her website at:

CarolABrown.com

www.ingramcontent.com/pod-product-compliance
Lightning Source LLC
Chambersburg PA
CBHW071543080526
44588CB00011B/1770